Enigmatic Petroglyphs
Deciphering Ancient Rock Art

Table of Contents

Chapter 1. Introduction

Unravel the mysteries of ancient civilizations with our Special Report: "Enigmatic Petroglyphs: Deciphering Ancient Rock Art". This intriguing report delves into the labyrinth of time, unveiling the secrets etched onto stones by our forebears. Through an engaging, layman-friendly narrative, we decode the encrypted tales and the elusive messages that have been left behind for us to discover. Our comprehensive exploration is not limited to a particular region, but spans across every continent, offering a global perspective on rock art. It doesn't matter whether you're an archaeology aficionado, history buff, art lover, or just a curious soul eager to delve into the ancient world; this report is a treasure chest waiting to be unlocked. Get ready to embark on a journey backwards in time where every turn reveals captivating marvels. This Special Report is more than just a purchase, it's your gateway to the dawn of human creativity and communication!

Chapter 2. The Art of Petroglyphs: An Introduction

To truly appreciate the art and mystery of petroglyphs, one must delve into the prehistoric era, an epoch that has left behind a treasure trove of ancient scripts etched on stone. Free from the constraints of language and yet rich in symbolism, these petroglyphs serve as a unique linguistical repository of our ancestors' emotions, observations, beliefs, and narratives.

2.1. Understanding Petroglyphs

Petroglyphs, derived from Greek roots 'petros' meaning 'stone' and 'glyphein' meaning 'to carve', basically denote carvings on rocks. They are prehistoric works of art that consist of images created by physically removing part of a rock surface to produce particular designs. The techniques of crafting these designs vary from pecking, scratching, abrading to incising using stone tools.

Various symbols, patterns, human and animal forms make up the general anthology of petroglyphs. The most intriguing element about these engravings lies in the abstract motifs and geometrical symbols, 'the language of lines', which are said to depict the cosmic universe or celestial events, as perceived by the ancient man.

A petroglyph's virtue and intrigue come not just from its artistry but also from its environmental context—the type of rock it has been etched on, its exact location and orientation, its relation to significant landmarks, and its relation to other petroglyphs. The study and evaluation of these aspects help us to understand the cultural importance and use of these sites to ancient societies.

2.2. Methods and Techniques of Petroglyph Making

The precise methodologies deployed for the creation of petroglyphs varied, depending on the tools available, the geological nature of the rocks, and the cultural aspirations of the artisans. Petroglyph creators primarily relied on rock pecking, whereby a pointed rock or bone was used to chip away the surface and reveal the lighter interior. Abrading or grinding rocks using a harder stone was another technique employed. Occasionally, incising or scratching was followed, especially when new metal tools were introduced.

The choice of rock for petroglyphs equally mattered; artists were selective about this aspect. Dark, patina-covered rocks, known as desert varnish, were preferred due to their ability to form a contrast with the lighter underneath surface. This exposed layer would then be further polished in some cases for enhancing the visibility of the design.

2.3. Thematic Elements and Decoding Meanings

The universe of petroglyphs showcases an array of themes—native animals, hunting scenes, celestial bodies, human figures, symbols and many intricate motifs, imbibed with inexplicit meanings to modern eyes. Through intensive research and interpretational acumen, analysts have tried to decode these icons into comprehensible narratives.

Many petroglyphs are suggested to represent supernatural phenomena or diety figures, indicative of the human need to understand, respect, and fear the wrath of nature and the cosmos. Glyphs of animals suggest the significance of hunting, while others might denote the spiritual aspect associated with the creature depicted. Certain petroglyphs indicate prehistoric humans' astronomical acumen, featuring celestial events accurately.

Complex iconic and geometric motifs mark a separate category of petroglyphs. These could represent maps, territorial markers, migration paths, or bear religious and cosmic implications as well. While concrete interpretations are challenging to achieve, they comprise an universally human symbolism - something that is understood without being said.

2.4. Petroglyphs Across Continents and Cultures

There is no dearth of diversity in this art form; petroglyphs are a global phenomenon with rich cultural varieties. From Europe's Atlantic Archipelago, showcasing the Late Neolithic symbols, to North America's Indigenous petroglyphs featuring abstracted animal forms, the range is astounding.

Asia's Indus Valley Civilization has yielded petroglyphs dated around 3300-1300 BCE, while Africa boasts rock art dating back to even 10,000 BCE in sites like Algeria's Tassili n'Ajjer. Australia's Aboriginal rock art is another fascinating treasure trove where the 'Bradshaw paintings' or 'Gwion Gwion' stand out, believed to be over 60,000 years old!

Every one of these geographical regions has unique stylistic variations, thematic preferences and socio-cultural implications, making the study of petroglyphs a mesmerizing journey across space and time.

As we delve deeper into this exploratory journey of petroglyphs in subsequent sections, you, as the reader, will be embarking on a voyage not just across the contours of physical landscapes, but also across the fascinating psychological terrain of our ancient forebears.

Hold on to your excitement and curiosity as we retreat into an era where rock art served as the primary form of storytelling and belief sharing, guiding us through the labyrinth of human history and culture.

Chapter 3. Symbols from the Stone Age

Stone Age societies, despite lacking formal writing systems, expressed their narratives through a complex library of symbols etched into the very fabric of Earth - the bedrock. These enduring testimonies, often labeled rudimentary due to their antiquity, are anything but. Their simplicity belies a rich tapestry of stories, beliefs, and traditions that provide us with a glimpse into the worldview of our most distant ancestors.

3.1. The Dawn of Symbolism

Before we delve into the petroglyphs of the Stone Age, it is important to understand the era from which these symbols emerge. The Stone Age is a period in human prehistory distinguished by the original development of stone tools, spanning more than 3 million years. Much of this age is categorized by technological and cultural milestones which saw mankind chart its first attempts at communication, manifesting in symbolic representation through art.

Evidence of early Stone Age art dates back to around 500,000 years, as seen in the zigzag engraving on a shell discovered in Java, Indonesia. However, a more concentrated period known as the Upper Paleolithic era, dating back to around 40,000 years ago, brought about an explosion of creative expression. Cave paintings, engravings, and sculptures were created with unprecedented sophistication. These artworks were laden with symbols - tangible reflections of intangible thoughts, abstract concepts, stories, and beliefs accumulated over countless generations.

3.2. Symbols: Forms and Functions

The range of Stone Age art symbols is as eclectic as the geographies they span and the cultures they represent. Animal figures, human forms, geometric patterns, and abstract designs - all held symbolic significance. The meaning of these signs shows the complexity of Stone Age thought, as well as the diverse ways the ancient artists sought to engage with and understand their world.

Animal figures were a dominant theme, immortalized in sprawling cave systems like those in Lascaux, France, or Altamira, Spain. These depictions often showcased a high degree of realism and detail, reflecting a keen observation of the natural world. They possibly represented hunting prayers, signifying strength or protection, or could be seen as a form of 'sympathetic magic', meant to control or appease these creatures.

Human forms, far less frequent and less detailed than animal depictions, were often highly stylized or exaggerated. Venus figurines, such as the Venus of Willendorf, are voluptuous female figures hypothesized to represent fertility or Earth's abundance. Anthropomorphic figures with part-human, part-animal features blur the lines between human and beast, as seen in 'The Sorcerer' in the Trois-Frères cave, France.

Geometry and abstract patterns, like dots, hashes, crosses, zigzags, and circles, punctuated caves and rock surfaces. Their ubiquity suggests shared symbolic meanings across diverse cultures. In some instances, these symbols may have denoted clan identities, demarcated territories, served as navigational guides, represented celestial bodies, or been mere artistic experiments.

3.3. Interpreting Ancient Symbols: Debates and Dilemmas

As rich as the world of Stone Age symbols is, their interpretation is a task fraught with difficulties. Unlike later periods with decipherable scripts, the Stone Age offers no Rosetta Stone. Decoding their meanings is a task reliant on careful observation of context, comparisons across time and place, and a deep understanding of ancient cultures and their understanding of the world. A feisty academic debate surrounds their interpretation, ranging from literal and utilitarian interpretations to deeply symbolic and transcendental ones.

3.4. Under the Microscope: Symbols as Cultural DNA

No one interpretation holds the key to Stone Age symbolism. Their elusive meanings, refracted through the lens of time, are probably an amalgamation of the practical and mystical. Each theory peels back another layer and provides a fresh perspective, which only adds to their enduring allure.

Symbolic literacy was akin to a cultural DNA, threading individuals into larger social units, giving a sense of shared identity, purpose, and understanding of the world. Thus, Stone Age symbols are perhaps not mere reflections of their environment, but also early expressions of mankind's inherent drive to question, communicate, and make sense of our existence.

In the grand scheme of human history, these symbols are our oldest ancestors, silently whispering across millennia and echoing the first-hand experiences of early Homo Sapiens. As posts in the ground, they mark the human journey from mere existence to self-expression and interpretation of our place in the universe.

3.5. Conclusion: Echoes from Yesteryears

Today, as we ponder over the enigmatic strokes and figures etched by stone onto stone, we hear whispers of stories that form the earliest chapters of our collective human experience. These symbols are the intertwined roots of art, language, and culture. Exploring them uncovers our primitive past while celebrating the human moment of self-consciousness and artistic expression.

This journey into Stone Age symbols has led us from the first glimmers of representation to the dawn of complex symbolic systems, encoding a multitude of meanings. While cloaked in the aura of mystery, these symbols remind us that, despite the passage of thousands of years, our ancestors were not so different from us. Their desires, fears, curiosities resonating through their art, providing a sense of continuity and reaffirming our shared humanity.

As we strive to further unravel these enigmatic inscriptions, we can look forward to uncovering more about our forebears' cognitive development, cultural practices, and societal structures. Each discovery is another piece in the vast jigsaw puzzle of human evolution, challenging us, just as our ancestors were, to pose questions, seek patterns, and ultimately, find meaning.

Chapter 4. Native American Petroglyphs: Decoding the Past

Human civilization, throughout history, has utilized various forms to express thoughts and ideas. However, one of the earliest known is perhaps the most fascinating - petroglyphs. These ancient carvings or peckings on rock surfaces are scattered across every populated continent, each enabling a unique peek into the past.

4.1. The Discovery

In North America, petroglyphs have been discovered in abundance, ranging from states like Nevada and Arizona to regions across the Canadian border. In fact, the rich legacy is evident in the over 100,000 recorded sites with hidden tales etched in stone. These designs vary in depth and complexity – some portraying simple, straightforward images like animals or humans, while others encompass metaphysical abstractions, likely symbolic and spiritual.

Tales were spun not only in lines, circles, and swirls etched into the rocks but also through their location. Often, they were drawn in places of special significance, like ancient hunting spots, sacred areas, or points of convergence in old trading routes. A magnifying glass over these rock canvasses reveals the life, beliefs, and experiences of Native American tribes, dated back several millennia.

4.2. The Spiritual Connection

Native American petroglyphs frequently depict mystical conversations with the spiritual world. The Hopi, Zuni, and Pueblo people considered these inscriptions an effort to communicate with their ancestors or the spiritual realm. Some images, recognizable as flora, fauna, and human figures, are interspersed with unknown symbols that presumably represent these spiritual interactions.

A fine example can be found in the Petrified Forest National Park, Arizona. Here, numerous petroglyphs depict supernatural entities known to the Hopi and Zuni as "Kachinas." Believed to be ancestral spirits, the Kachinas are often drawn adorned with headdresses and masks, signifying their esteemed status in the tribal belief system. A discerning observation of these offerings on stone provides rich insights into the ancient Native American relationship with the spiritual realm.

4.3. Interpreting the Symbols

The task of decoding these petroglyphs is akin to deciphering a lost language. To date, no definitive key has been discovered, and the meaning of many images remains elusive.

However, patterns have been discerned. Interpreting petroglyphs often involves understanding the social and cultural context in which they were created. Certain figures, like bison or deer, clearly denote essential game animals, while regional flora may symbolize seasonal changes or medicinal practices.

What continues to baffle scholars are the purely abstract symbols. Spirals, zigzag lines, concentric circles, and humanoid figures with no apparent features are still cloaked in obscurity. Several theories suggest they might be symbolic representations of shamanic visions, celestial events, tribal boundaries, or even expressions of abstract thought.

4.4. The Petroglyphs of Writing-On-Stone

Writing-On-Stone, a provincial park in Alberta, Canada, is a significant Native American heritage site known for its abundant petroglyphs and pictographs. This sandy prairie valley, punctuated by towering sandstone monoliths, has drawn both indigenous visitors and historians alike to study the hundreds of rock art images distributed throughout the park.

The art at Writing-On-Stone predominantly features humans, footprints, animals, and geometric figures. These are often interpreted as records of significant events, mythology, and everyday happenings of the ancestral Blackfoot people. The park presents an invaluable chronicle for researchers, enabling them to delve deeper into the cultural, social, and spiritual life of the once thriving Native American civilization.

4.5. Unresolved Mysteries

Despite noteworthy progress in the interpretation of petroglyphs, scholars have yet to unlock the full narrative of the enigmatic rock art. The quest for knowledge continues, with archaeologists, anthropologists, and historians joining hands to solve the knotted riddles still lurking in the petroglyphs.

Native American petroglyphs present a unique amalgamation of culture, spirituality, and history imprinted in stone. The distinct chronicles etched onto rock faces have traversed time, surviving weathering, vandalism, and neglect. As we continue to decipher these ancient inscriptions, let's safeguard these sites as invaluable links to our human past and testimony to the complexity of our ancestors' lives. With every discovered petroglyph comes a new piece to the grand jigsaw puzzle - the history of human communication and creativity.

Chapter 5. Imprints of the Ancient East: Asia's Rock Art

Asia, home to many great ancient civilizations, is a treasure trove of historical rock art waiting to be deciphered. This extensive region, stretching from Turkey to Japan, plays host to numerous sites adorned with petroglyphs, pictographs, and other forms of rock art, encapsulating myriad stories of the stages of human growth and ingenuity.

5.1. The Neolithic Hunters: Petroglyphs of Siberia

As one of the most remote corners of Eastern Asia, Siberia remains an unexplored haven harboring ancient mysteries. The petroglyphs etched onto the region's vast stone canvases furnish archaeological testimonies of the region's resilient residents who once braved the harsh Siberian winters. Hundreds of such sites grace the eastern shores of Lake Baikal, the world's oldest and deepest freshwater lake.

These petroglyphs predominantly feature striking images of wild animals, hunters, and weapons, indicative of the inhabitants' connection with nature, hunting, and their struggle for survival in an unforgiving environment. Among the detailed depictions, researchers often discover anthropomorphic figures, possibly indicative of early deities or perhaps tribal leaders. While their exact syntax remains a mystery, these symbols provide vital information about the beginnings of human worldview and religious beliefs.

5.2. Enigmatic Inscriptions of India

Moving southwards from Siberia's icy plains, we land on the rich, vibrant culture of the Indian subcontinent. The sites at Bhimbetka, Hazaribagh, and Kerala offer a canvas of rock art imagery spanning over several millennia.

Bhimbetka, with more than 700 rock shelters adorned with petroglyphs, is known for its artistic excellence and sheer variety. These depictions vary from everyday life scenes, rituals, and communal dances to large, animal forms suggestive of the Mesolithic period's mystic invocation. Further North, rock art sites in Hazaribagh showcase enigmatic inscriptions and unique geometric forms, believed to be associated with significant ancient rituals.

The rock art of Kerala, contrasting to the northern petroglyphs, is marked by its obsession with human figures. Numerous depictions of male and female forms gracing the rock surfaces, often holding weapons, suggest a society steeped in social hierarchy, warfare, and fruitfulness rituals.

5.3. The Western Xia Kingdom: Rock Art of China

The petroglyphs found in China's Ningxia province point towards the life and times of the Western Xia Kingdom (1038-1227 AD). Famously known as "Helan Mountain Ghost Face", these rock arts are distinctive in their style, predominantly showcasing sun, moon, animals, and masked figures.

These ghostly masks, featuring wide mouths and protruding eyes, are believed to signify superiority or divine power. The sun and moon depictions possibly represent the dual concept omnipresent in Chinese philosophy, symbolizing balance and harmony.

5.4. Geometrical Complexity: Petroglyphs of Korea

The Bangudae Petroglyphs in South Korea provide a unique take on rock art by emphasizing geometrical composition. Containing representations of hunting, rituals, and animals alongside mystical whales, these petroglyphs uniquely showcase marine life.

Believed to be engraved around 7,000 years ago, the Korean rock art indicates societal development with communal hunting representations and elaborate whale hunting scenes suggesting a shift towards a fishing economy. The precision and detail within this art form remind us of the inherent creativity our ancestors possessed.

5.5. The Enigma of the Jōmon: Japan's Cherished Heritage

Lastly, the Jōmon-period rock art of Japan provides a glimpse into the cultural complexity of the island settlers, who lived in Japan from 14,000–300 B.C. The rock art portrays an assortment of images ranging from human figures, sea animals to complex abstract patterns.

Arguably one of the most fascinating elements within Jōmon petroglyphs is the predominant boar imagery, believed to be interlinked with hunting practices and ceremonial aspects of Jōmon culture. The ethereal abstract patterns suggest a complex symbolic language and have been linked by scholars to intricate Jōmon pottery designs.

This captivating eastward journey through Asia's rock art underlines the universal human inclination towards creativity and communication. These timeless etchings remind us of their creators' lives and cultures, providing us with invaluable windows into the distant past. Each petroglyph, a silent storyteller, continues to echo untold tales lying at the core of our shared human narrative. While we may not fully decipher the cryptic messages they hold, these stony archives continue to offer awe-inspiring glimpses into the dawn of human history.

Chapter 6. Africa's Petroglyphic Panorama: From the Sahara to the Cape

Engulfing a significant portion of the planet, Africa—a cradle of human civilization, offers a vast and rich canvas to the saga of primitive human expressions etched in stone. From the serene landscapes of the Sahara to the lush biodiversity of the Cape, the continental expanse hides innumerable mysteries waiting to be deciphered.

6.1. The Sahara's Timeless Canvases

As we cast our gaze upon the endless stretches of the Sahara desert, little would one suspect this arid landscape had been, thousands of years ago, home to human life and verdant vegetation. This extraordinary past is evidenced by the intriguing patterns and figures scribed onto the fortress-like cliffs of the Tassili n'Ajjer mountains and Wadi Mathendous.

A kaleidoscope of antelopes, giraffes, swimming humans, and intricate symbols spanning over 10,000 years reveal a periodic transformation from the hunter-gatherer lifestyle to adoptive farming practices, a testament to our ancestors' resilience and adaptability. Interwoven within the depictions of wild fauna are interpretations of celestial events, alluding to our forebears' intriguingly comprehensive understanding of astronomical phenomena.

6.2. Nile's Rosetta of Rock Art

Next, we chart a course along the Nile, bearing witness to the archaeological treasures of the Pharaonic age where Egypt's forefathers have imprinted their legacy in both the corporal form of the pyramids and the ethereal realm of rock art.

Contrary to their counterparts, Egyptian petroglyphs embraced symbolism and faith over literal manifestations. Animal iconography - elaborate falcons, poised lions, and surreally endowed hybrid creatures - were enshrined as deities, demarcating a shift to a structured religious order. Moreover, these pictorial testimonials provide an irreplaceable link to the evolution of the sophisticated hieroglyphic script.

6.3. The Enigma of Chad's Dabous Giraffes

We then traverse towards the heart of Africa, to the terrestrial wonder of the Sahara. Chad's Dabous region is home to what could arguably be the world's largest petroglyph - a pair of perfectly executed giraffes towering above the plateau.

The artistic finesse involved in carving the animals' intricate patterns, down to the minutest details, proves to be a marvelous testimony to the prowess and artistic ingenuity of our ancestors nearly 7000 years ago. Observations of slight variances in the shading and the finesse of the carving style hint at a possible multi-generation project.

6.4. The Terrains of Twyfelfontein, Namibia

Our next stop is the crimson sands of Namibia, where the Twyfelfontein valley stands as an open petroglyph museum. Venerated with a UNESCO World Heritage Site status, the valley bears the unique distinction of having one of the highest concentrations of rock engravings in Africa.

The predominant depictions here are of bushmen's interactions with the environment, replete with rhinoceroses, elephants, giraffes, and human footsteps. Often clubbed with the animal figures are symbols thought to represent the shamanic spirit world, reflecting the then-prevalent culture's deep-rooted spiritualism.

6.5. South Africa's Cape Landscapes

Finally, let's journey to the tip of the continent, where South Africa's diverse geological landscaping vividly mirrors the diversity of its rock art. From Bushman's Kloof and Cederberg mountains to uKhahlamba-Drakensberg, the narratives shift between the physical and metaphysical realms.

While the San bushmen chronicled their interactions with nature and epic hunting scenes, the later KhoiSan people, noted for their pastoral lifestyle, etched carvings of domesticated animals, altering the narrative to record changes in societal structures and lifestyle.

Africa's Petroglyphic Panorama is not only a testament to changing environment, society, and beliefs but a testament to the human spirit and its continual evolution. From the stark deserts to the fertile valleys, the tale of humanity curated in stone spans millennia, telling an ever-evolving epic of survival, wisdom, spirituality, and innate artistry.

Chapter 7. Echoes of the Ancestors: Europe's Time-Imprisoned Narratives

European rock art, scattered from Scandinavia to Iberia and from the British Isles to the Ural Mountains, cartwheels across a stunning array of eras and cultures. Its monumental diversity makes it a stimulant for scholarly endeavors and a visual feast for enthusiasts.

7.1. The Palette of Time: Evolution of Rock Art Techniques

It is crucial to first venture into the assortment of techniques employed by our ancestors, painting a vibrant panorama of time. Early rock art, dating back to before 10000 BCE, were primarily etchings known as 'petroglyphs'. Carved out from the bedrock using stone tools, these early illustrations were mainly of hand-prints, powerful animals like mammoths, and abstract symbols.

With the ending of the last Ice Age, the palette expanded. As Europe's landscape metamorphosed into forests and plains, people began to represent game animals such as deer and aurochs. 'Pictographs' or painted rock art, became increasingly prevalent with the use of natural pigments like ochre and charcoal, giving life to these images in shades of red, black, yellow and white.

7.2. Mystical Shamans and Their Esoteric Illustrations

Shamanism, a belief system based on intermediaries communicating with the spirit world, was pervasive in early Europe. Some researchers propose that shamans, potentially under the influence of hallucinogens conveyed their spiritual journeys and practices through rock art. Esoteric symbols resembling geometric patterns, trances, and shamanic transformations intersperse the rock faces along with recognizable fauna, lend credence to this hypothesis.

7.3. Stories Encased in Stone: Depicting Daily Life

Moving from the abstract to the concrete, rock art began to demonstrate an elementary form of narrative, perhaps society's earliest chronicles. Scenes from hunting and gathering, fishing, and warfare were etched onto the rock surfaces. Human figures, though stylized, became a part of these visual narrations, adding layers to our understanding of societal structures and norms during those times.

7.4. Bronze Age Blossoms: Celestial Symbols and Complex Narratives

Towards the end of the Neolithic Age and the onset of the Bronze Age, technological advancements began to reflect in the rock art. Metallurgical developments were suggested by depictions of bronze weapons and tools. Mysterious 'sun-boat' motifs, that some researchers interpret as cosmic voyages, appeared across Scandinavia, while across Ireland and Britain, petroglyphs of spirals and concentric circles became prevalent, hinting at possible astronomical interpretations.

7.5. Cryptic Writings: Arrival of Runes and Ogham

The arrival of the Iron Age paved the way for initial attempts at written communication. Across Scandinavia, Rune scripts began to accompany the pictorial depictions, the enigmatic symbols found engraved on rune stones. In contrast, across Ireland and Britain, Ogham engravings started appearing on stone monuments. Such early alphabets give fascinating insight into a transitional era when ancient cultures were moving towards structured writing systems.

7.6. Tracing the Echoes of Ancestors: Decoding Rock Art

Deciphering rock art is not just about revealing an ancient sketchbook; it's about unpicking the knotted threads of time to reveal an evolving human story. Archaeologists and historians still grapple with discrepancies and ambiguities in the interpretation of rock art owing to its subjective nature. However, using modern tools such as digital imaging and radiocarbon dating, we can contextually ground and interpret these intricate symbols more accurately than ever.

Despite its enigmatic characteristic, deciphering rock art presents not just a challenge but a promise. A promise of unfolding a deeper, untold story of our past that's hidden beneath time's hardened crust. Through the echoes of our ancestors inscribed on stone, we seek to understand ourselves - our genesis, our journey, and perhaps even, our future.

In conclusion, European rock art, beautifully cryptic and astonishingly diverse, holds an invaluable key to mankind's past. It is a testament of humanity's unbroken connection with the natural world, the spiritual realm, and each other, through boundless time and space. Each stroke, each symbol calls us to keep looking, keep decoding, as we strive to listen to these timeless narratives. These are narratives that are not only worth hearing but are essential in our collective quest to understand who we are, where we come from and what shaped us through millennia.

Chapter 8. Aboriginal Australia: Art from the Dreamtime

In Australia's remote wilderness, hidden amidst unforgiving terrain and inhospitable climates, lie one of the world's oldest surviving testimonies of human expression. The Aboriginal rock art silhouetted against age-old cliffs whisper tales from times immemorial, long before written language came into existence.

8.1. The Lore of Dreamtime

A significant aspect of Aboriginal culture is the Dreamtime, or 'The Dreaming' - an era beyond the scope of our temporal understanding. This is not a single point in time, but rather, it connotes the timeless landscape of the Aboriginal spiritual ethos.

The Dreamtime has been transferred across generations via various media, the most popular forms being storytelling, ceremonial dances, and art, inclusive of the rock illustrations explored in this chapter. This art embodied their profound connection with the land, an aspect that has played a pivotal role throughout the Dreamtime.

Rock art was not merely an expression but a way of life and communication medium for the Aborigines. Each piece conveys a story from their mythology or documents their daily life, their triumphs and tribulations, their relationship with the land, and the animals that shared it with them.

8.2. The Enigma of Artistic Styles

Aboriginal petroglyphs are far from being one homogenous entity.

They vary dramatically geographically and temporally, each region casting its distinctive style and palette onto these ancient canvases. Some sites are characterized by large, monochromatic human and animal figures – a style referred to as the Dynamic Figures Style. Conversely, other sites feature complex motifs of geometric shapes and patterns, known as the Panaramittee style.

The Dynamic Figures Style is distinguished by action-filled illustrations holding spears or boomerangs, arrayed with adornments like headdresses and waistbands. On the other hand, the Panaramittee style is typified by the engraving of small, track-like motifs of emus, kangaroos, and humans, neatly executed into the hard rock surfaces.

8.3. Temporal Echoes: Ancient to Contemporary Art

It is the longevity and continuity of the rock art tradition that makes Aboriginal art exceptional. The Bradshaw or Gwion Gwion art of the Kimberley region dating back some 20,000 years serves as an exquisite example. These elegant human figures adorned with ornate regalia stand as silent witnesses to a long-forgotten past.

Contrasting with these are contemporary public art forms, such as the graffiti-style paintings in Sydney's Domain, where Aboriginal identity is expressed against the backdrop of modern living.

8.4. Interpreting Symbols: Wandjina and X-ray Art

Wandjina are the Cloud and Rain Spirits from the Dreamtime, depicted in rock art across the Kimberley region. These distinctive figures appear as large, wide-eyed creatures without mouths, surrounded by a halo-like structure, often in correlation with weather patterns.

On the other side of the stylistic spectrum is X-ray art, a unique Aboriginal artistic style predominant in Arnhem Land. Characterized by the internal organs and skeletal structures of humans and animals, X-ray art reveals a deep understanding of anatomy and reinforces the intricate connection between the physical and spiritual realms.

8.5. Preserving a Legacy

The legacy that Aboriginal art carries is undoubtedly priceless. However, this cultural treasure is threatened by natural weathering, vandalism, and industrial development. Recognising the urgency of their preservation, conservational initiatives are gaining momentum. Australia's government, alongside various institutions, is investing efforts and funding in protective measures, like constructing barriers and offering guided tours to visitors, ensuring minimal interference with these relics.

Each stroke etched onto stone all those millennia ago echoes stories - an eternal testament to the marvel of human imagination and ingenuity. Aboriginal rock art empowers us to listen to these tales, inviting us to imagine a once populated world echoing with the rhythms of a bygone era. Here, in the silence of the centuries, we find our connection with the ancient members of our human family, reminding us that however far we have come, roots draw us back to the cradle of human civilization and expression.

Chapter 9. South America's Enigmatic Stone Scribes

South America, a land known for its rich culture, vibrant history, and wild geography, is also home to a magnificent collection of ancient rock art. The petroglyphs form an intricate web of stories, etched onto stones by ancient civilization, and offer us an insight into their way of life, beliefs, and knowledge of their environment.

9.1. Prehistoric Petroglyphs

Dating back as far as 10,000 years, these petroglyphs represent not just physical objects but the spiritual, astronomical, and geographic conceptions of the prehistoric inhabitants of this landscape. You can see the circles, spirals, and complex geometric patterns in these sites that are spread across the continent - Argentina, Brazil, Chile, Colombia, and Peru, to name a few. While these patterns might seem enigmatic, ongoing research works are shedding light on the sophisticated understanding of these ancient civilizations.

One such site is the Cueva de las Manos in Argentina. A UNESCO World Heritage Site, this 'Cave of Hands' showcases numerous human hand stencils. These are not just marks of human presence but narrative of the passage of time, with radiocarbon dating shows that these images were created over a span of about 1,300 years.

9.2. Mystical Figures and Animal Depictions

Steer away from abstract shapes, and another widespread motif in South American rock art is the depiction of humans and animals. Researchers believe that these carvings were often associated with hunting rituals or were offerings for successful hunting trips.

In the outskirts of Rio de Janeiro, Brazil, you'll find the largest collection of rock art in the Americas at Serra da Capivara National Park. The park boasts over 30,000 prehistoric paintings. Many depict hunting scenes, ceremonies, and depictions of day-to-day life, bearing testament to the region's early human inhabitance.

Amidst Andean skylines of Peru, lie the mysterious figures of Toro Muerto. Spread across a stretch of four kilometres, are caves adorned with over 5000 volcanic rocks featuring an array of carved images. From human figures, geometrical designs, to an assortment of fauna like condors, snakes, and llamas – the range of depictions suggests a complex socio-cultural milieu.

9.3. Astronomical Knowledge

An intriguing aspect of South American rock art is the representation of celestial bodies and events. This reflects the importance that astronomical observation held for these societies, perhaps for agricultural, ritualistic, or navigational purposes.

The Calçoene megalithic observatory, popularly termed as 'Amazon Stonehenge,' is an archaeological site in Brazil, widely recognized for its sophisticated astronomical alignment. This complex structure constitutes a set of granite blocks aligned precisely with the winter solstice, thereby offering insights into the extensive knowledge of prehistoric people about the celestial orbits.

9.4. Mythical Creatures and Supernatural Beings

Their spiritual beliefs formed a significant part of these ancient civilizations' lives, and this is intricately depicted in the petroglyphs. The engravings provide a window into their mythology, showcasing a panoply of mythical creatures, shamans, and otherworldly beings.

One must mention the San Agustín Archaeological Park in Colombia, holding the largest collection of religious monuments and megalithic sculptures in South America. An amalgamation of animal and human figures, these monumental statues illustrate a vivid pantheon of gods revered by the people of this ancient culture.

9.5. Conclusion

The rock art in South America provides profound and diverse insights into the rich history, culture, and sociology of its ancient residents, much of which remains enigmatic due to the vanishing of their creators. However, with each passing day, scholars and archaeologists decipher one more stroke, one more line that brings us closer to understanding our ancestors.

In the next chapter, we will go down under to explore the vast sites of ancient petroglyphs in Australia, where the oldest known rock art in the world awaits our perusal.

Chapter 10. Tracing Historical Ages through Petroglyphs

The study of rock art, or petroglyphs, provides a fascinating window into the past, giving us a sense of the worldviews and creative impulses of our ancestors. Petroglyphs are more than just decorative or symbolic sketches carved onto rock surfaces; they are significant sources of historical information that can help us reconstruct past human cultures and periods.

10.1. The Dawn of Petroglyphs

Petroglyphs first appear during the Upper Paleolithic period (circa 40,000 to 10,000 BCE) in Europe and Asia. The oldest known petroglyphs in Europe, located in El Castillo cave in Spain, date back to circa 40,000 BCE. These enigmatic images, drawn by early humans, depict a myriad of life forms, including various animals and human forms.

Moving eastward, the vast central plateau of Iran is home to several sites with Petroglyphs dating back to circa 40,000 BCE, suggesting a broad distribution of early rock art. The carved patterns here highlight hunting scenes, animals like horses, bulls, and much more, allowing us to steal glimpses into the cultures they came from.

10.2. Unveiling the Neolithic Age

As we move into the Neolithic period (circa 10,000 – 4,500 BCE), the themes displayed in petroglyphs evolved. The shift from hunting-gathering societies to settled farming cultures significantly impacted the content and distribution of rock art.

One of the significant Neolithic petroglyph sites is found in the high desert of New Mexico – the Three Rivers Petroglyph site. This site houses more than 21,000 glyphs, with depictions of humans, flora, fauna, geometric motifs, and more. These etchings embody the transition to a more settled society and the social and environmental experiences of an evolving culture.

In Scandinavia, the petroglyphs from this period, found at sites like Tanum and Alta, are acclaimed worldwide. Radiating with vibrant scenes of hunting, farming, and navigation, they reveal the community's sophisticated knowledge, skills, and societal norms in these areas.

10.3. Petroglyphs in the Bronze Age

With the advent of the Bronze Age (circa 3,300 – 1,200 BCE), petroglyphs show further complexity and diversity. The famous petroglyphs at Tanum in Sweden, created during this period, include depictions of ships, people, animals, and complex scenes of rituals or mythology. These indicate the importance of seafaring, the relationships between communities, and the spiritual beliefs of Bronze Age people.

The Val Camonica rock art in Italy, a UNESCO World Heritage site, houses over 200,000 petroglyphs. These rock carvings depict themes linked to agriculture, warfare, and domestic life, showing the evolving dynamics of human societies during the Bronze Age.

10.4. Transitioning into the Iron Age

The Iron Age (approx. 1,200 BCE onwards) saw increased contact between different cultures due to technological advancements and expanding trade, and this is reflected in petroglyphs from this time.

Comparatively more recent, the majority of Iron Age petroglyphs across the globe mark the evolution of language, recording the early development of alphabets and written script. The petroglyphs at Wadi Rum in modern-day Jordan bear ancient Thamudic and Nabatean inscriptions, functioning as a kind of message board through the ages.

Over in North America, the Hohokam Petroglyphs located in Arizona depict spirals, animals, humans, and geometric figures portraying a vibrant culture enriched by symbology and ceremony.

10.5. The Gift of Petroglyphs

Through the ages, petroglyphs offer us an invaluable insight into our ancestral cultures and their perceptions of the world around them. By studying these ancient and fascinating etchings, we gain immense understanding and appreciation of the myriad of human experiences and expressions transgressing temporal boundaries.

They act as silent witnesses, communicating historical eras' nuances and shifts in human experience over tens of thousands of years. These petroglyphs, our early ancestors' communications, usher us through history, allowing us to trace the chronology and evolutionary aspects of human civilization.

As we continue to uncover, evaluate, and decode petroglyphs, we must realize their value in understanding how societies have shaped and been shaped by the world around them. And in doing so, we can gain a deeper knowledge of our past and a broader perspective of who we are today.

Chapter 11. Interpretation and Conservation: Preserving Our Ancient Artistic Heritage

Deep within the recesses of early human history, our ancestors began to express their experiences and insights by inscribing symbols on stone canvases. These petroglyphs, as they are known today, served as parchment for primitive societies to record their histories, express spiritual revelations, and share knowledge across generations. Understanding the finer nuances of their interpretation, then preserving them for future generations, forms the bedrock of this exploration.

11.1. Interpreting Petroglyphs: A Linguistic Conundrum

Unraveling the meanings behind the petroglyphs is akin to deciphering an ancient, forgotten language. As researchers, we face numerous roadblocks on that path. Chief among them is that petroglyphs most often lack a one-to-one correspondence with words in modern languages. Their interpretation can also be dependent on unpredictable factors, such as the petroglyph's orientation, the light cast upon it, even the petroglyph's relation to other symbols nearby.

One popular methodology among archaeologists involves comparisons with iconography found in ethnographic sources or historical texts. For example, petroglyphs depicting hunting scenes might suggest a society's reliance on particular animal species or even symbolize mythical or spiritual narratives.

Another common method is to analyze the context in which a petroglyph was made. The ecological systems, cultural influences, historical periods, and geographical considerations all play a crucial role in this strategy.

11.2. The Role of Indigenous Knowledge

Indigenous societies can often provide invaluable insights into the interpretation of ancient rock art. These societies often preserve traditions, beliefs, and knowledge systems through the oral tradition or folklore that directly relate to the rock art. Anchoring our interpretations in the wisdom of these societies can help bridge the cultural gap and promote a deeper understanding of the pictorial narratives we seek to decipher.

The San people of the Kalahari, for example, explained individual elements in rock paintings discovered in South Africa. Their explanations stemmed from a place of deep cultural knowledge, illustrating a complex spiritual realm that modern scholars might struggle to appreciate without such invaluable insights.

11.3. The Challenges of Conservation

Just as crucial as the interpretation of petroglyphs is the challenge of their conservation. These ancient works of art are at the mercy of natural elements, such as wind, water, and sunlight, which contribute to their gradual decay. Beyond natural factors, human influence, through vandalism or neglect, has also significantly threatened these invaluable pieces of human heritage.

Preserving these sites involves multiple tasks, from controlling visitor access, employing protective measures such as shelters, to ongoing monitoring and maintenance.

11.4. The Role of Technology in Petroglyph Conservation

Given the sheer number of petroglyph sites worldwide and their often remote locations, harnessing modern technology has been crucial in our conservation efforts. For example, digital photography and 3D scanning allow for high-resolution replicas to be created for study, without the need for physical access that might harm the originals.

Another example is the advanced imaging technology such as Reflectance Transformation Imaging (RTI), which aids archaeologists to perceive details that are invisible to the naked eye.

11.5. Sustainable Tourism and Education

Promoting sustainable tourism and imparting education form another vital aspect of petroglyph conservation. Well-managed tourist visits not only help raise awareness and appreciation for rock art but also generate income vital for maintaining and protecting these sites.

Equally vital is educational outreach, which increases public understanding about the cultural significance of these sites, and the importance of their protection. Emphasizing the historical and cultural value of petroglyphs can help cultivate a sense of responsibility towards their preservation.

In concluding, the study, interpretation, and conservation of petroglyphs reveal a truly awe-inspiring facet of our shared human heritage. As the ciphers to our collective past evolve, new technologies and methodologies are emerging to aid us in preserving ancient artistic expressions. And with each symbol deciphered, each narrative interpreted, we come a step closer to understanding the enigmatic lives of our ancient forebears.

Printed in Dunstable, United Kingdom